On A Tight Rope

On A Tight Rope

BY ANN AND CHARLES MORSE
PHOTOGRAPHS BY STUART BAY

EMC CORPORATION
ST. PAUL, MINNESOTA

Library of Congress Cataloging in Publication Data

Morse, Ann.
    On a tight rope.

    (Their Just like you, just like me)
    SUMMARY: Inexperienced in climbing, eight-year-old Liza fearfully anticipates a family rock-climbing expedition.

    [1. Rock climbing—Fiction]   I. Morse, Charles, joint author.
II. Bay, Stuart, illus.   III. Title.
PZ7.M845820n   [Fic]   73-14685
ISBN 0-88436-031-8
ISBN 0-88436-032-6 (pbk.)

Copyright 1973 by EMC Corporation
All rights reserved. Published 1973

No part of this publication can be reproduced, stored in a retrieval system, or transmitted in any form or by any means; electronic, mechanical, photo copying, recording, or otherwise, without the permission of the publisher.

Published by EMC Corporation
180 East Sixth Street
St. Paul, Minnesota 55101
Printed in the United States of America
0987654321

JUST LIKE YOU, JUST LIKE ME
MAX-I-FISH
ON A TIGHT ROPE
LOST AND FOUND
FORWARD ROLL

1988048

Liza, Ann and Peter Klein asked their Mom and Dad to take them to the river falls. The river falls had the best rocks for climbing. Some of the rocks were high and very hard to climb. Everyone in the city said so.

The kids asked their Mom and Dad many times. And many times they said no. But this week they said yes. "We will go on Saturday," Dad said. Mom agreed and the plans were made.

Dad bought a new rope. It was very good for rock climbing. Mr. Klein knew that the family could use the rope at the river falls. Ann and Peter were very good at climbing. They knew how to use a rope. They could climb the highest rocks. But Liza was just learning to climb. She had never used a rope. And she had never tried to climb the highest rocks.

Ann and Peter thought the rope was great. Liza was a little afraid when she saw it. But she didn't tell anyone. She wanted to learn to climb rocks as well as her brother and sister. So she pretended to be just as glad about the rope as Ann and Peter.

8

Dad showed Liza how to use the rope. He told her what they would do when it was time to climb the high rocks. Mom and Ann and Peter helped Liza too. They showed Liza pictures of some of the rocks they had climbed. They told her how much fun it was to climb to the very top.

Liza thought about Saturday. She was afraid of climbing. The high rocks scared her. She was only eight years old. Ann and Peter were older and they knew how to climb. Liza wondered if she should tell her family that she was afraid. She thought and thought about it. But she said nothing. She wanted to go on the trip very much.

Finally it was Saturday morning. Ann and Peter got up first. Liza was a little slow about getting up. Mom and Dad were the last up. It was hard to wait for them to get ready. Even the cartoons didn't seem funny.

Soon everyone was up and each one had a job. Mom made the breakfast and the picnic lunch. Ann and Peter got their things ready. They found the rope and the other things they would need. "What about our knapsacks, Mom?" Peter asked.

"We don't need them," Mom said. "We are only going for the day."

11

Liza helped Mom pack the lunch. She helped her Dad take things out to the car. Liza wondered if she should tell her Dad that she was afraid. Maybe he would say something to help her feel better. But Liza did not say anything. Maybe at the falls she would be brave.

At last everything was ready. The kids jumped into the car and tried to wait. It was so hard to wait while Mom and Dad got those last few things. Finally, the Kleins were on their way.

Ann saw the park sign first. "We are at the river falls. I can see the rocks from here," she shouted. Before the car was unpacked, Ann and Peter ran to climb the rocks. "Look at the river from here," Peter shouted from a rock.

"I'm coming, I'm coming," Ann called up to him.

"Hey you climbers, get down here," Dad called to them. "We have to unload the car first and find a picnic spot."

Ann and Peter ran down the rocks and helped. "Okay. Are we ready now, Dad?" Peter asked.

17

"Let's start at the rocks by the sign," Peter said. "Those look like a cinch," he added. Peter tied the rope around a big rock. He used the rope to climb up the rocks. "Look, it works," yelled Peter.

Ann and Liza ran to Peter. When their Mom and Dad caught up, the kids were climbing the rocks. "Come on, Mom and Dad," Liza called. It was easier than she thought. Even when her foot slipped, her hands felt tight on the rocks. "It's fun," Liza shouted. She was glad she was there.

Up and down the rocks. Near the water. Up the hill. Climbing carefully around edges. The Kleins were having a good time. Dad kept close watch on Liza. Mom and the other two kids went first. Each rock got harder to climb. Liza was very pleased with herself. She almost forgot that she was getting tired.

"This will be the test," Ann said as they reached a very steep hill. Liza took a deep breath. Could she ever climb it? Liza felt as if she were going to cry. She was so good on the other rocks. But Liza knew that this was a hard rock to climb.

"That might be a little hard for some of us," Dad said to Ann.

"Let's try it anyway," Peter said.

Mom and Dad talked together. Then they asked for a vote. "Those in favor of going up this hill, say yes," Dad said.

"Yes!" said Ann quickly.

Peter voted "Yes," too.

And Liza said, "Yes." But she said it very softly.

"Let's go," said Mom. She patted Liza on the back.

Now they had to use the rope. Liza started up with the others. Ann led the way. Peter went behind her. Liza and Dad were last. The first few rocks were easy. There was a resting place part way up the hill. While Liza and Dad rested, the others began the steep part. Ann hung over a rock and laughed. "Let's have our picnic here," she called.

Liza and Dad had to work hard to keep up with the others. The rocks got sharper and higher. Peter climbed and climbed. He was almost at the top. Finally Ann and Peter and Mom climbed over the top of the rock. "Hurray!" they called. "It's great up here. You can see for miles."

"Hurray yourself," called Dad. "We will be there in a minute." He thought that might make Liza feel better. Liza thought her feet didn't feel as steady as they did on the other rocks. And her hands felt hot and tired. "Will I ever get to the top?" Liza asked herself. Ann and Peter and Mom seemed far away.

"You can do it," Dad said. "Tell yourself you can do it, Liza."

Liza didn't think so. 'No, I can't do it. I'm too tired. Let's go back down."

But her Dad said no. "The others are at the top. We will be there too. Just keep at it, Liza." And they both climbed. Each step was hard for Liza. She was hot and tired and afraid.

"Come on, Liza. You can do it," Ann shouted.

"Do it like I did," Peter called.

"We know you can make it, Liza," Mom said. "You are doing a good job. Keep your feet firm on each rock." Dad went in front of Liza. He climbed up first. Then he helped Liza use the rope to climb the rocks. Now Liza was all alone on the rocks.

Everyone thought she could make it. But Liza didn't feel so sure. "How could Peter get up there? Why is it so hard for me?" she wondered. Liza began to cry.

"Come on Liza! You can do it," Dad called. Liza wiped her face. She looked up at the rocks. She saw all the others at the top. Liza felt her teeth close tight together.

"I'll do it," Liza said. "I'll make it to the top." She gripped the rocks with her hands. With all the strength left in her legs, she climbed. And climbed. She kept on climbing until her feet touched the rock at the top.

29

"You made it, Liza! Just three more steps and you will be up!" Dad was smiling. He reached for Liza's hand. Mom took the other hand. Liza was on top.

Liza cried and laughed at the same time. "I made it. By myself, I made it." Liza jumped around. "I made it to the top. I'm here."